Harry Potter™

RAVENCLAW
HOUSE PRIDE

RAVENCLAW™

BATSFORD

WIZARDING WORLD

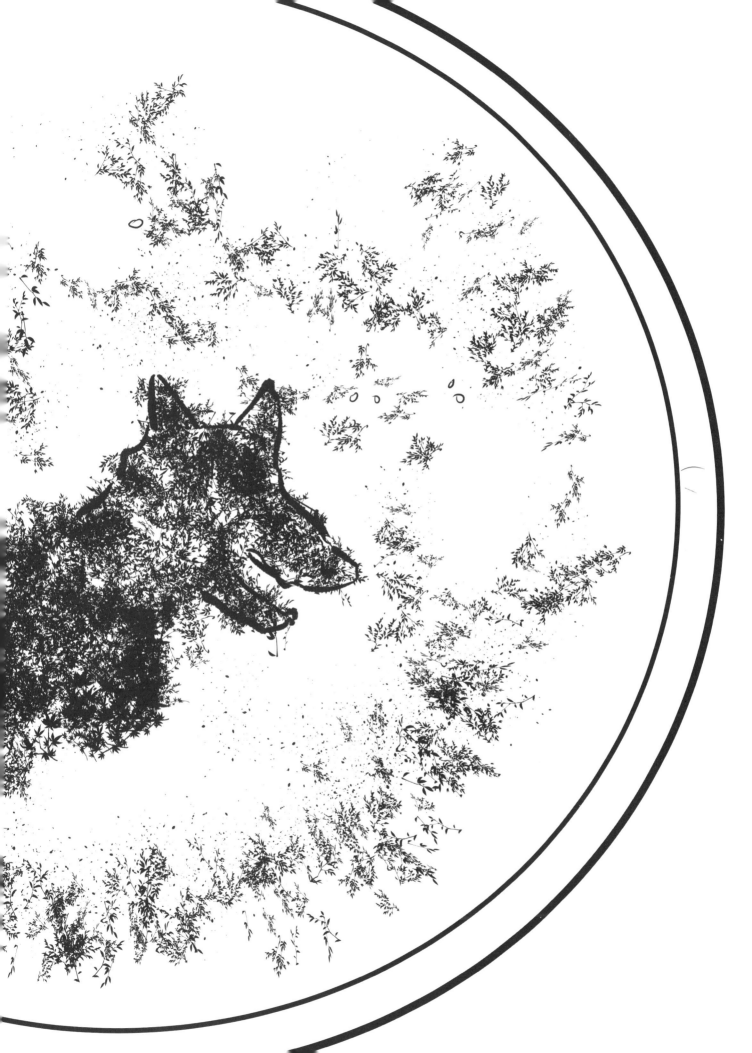

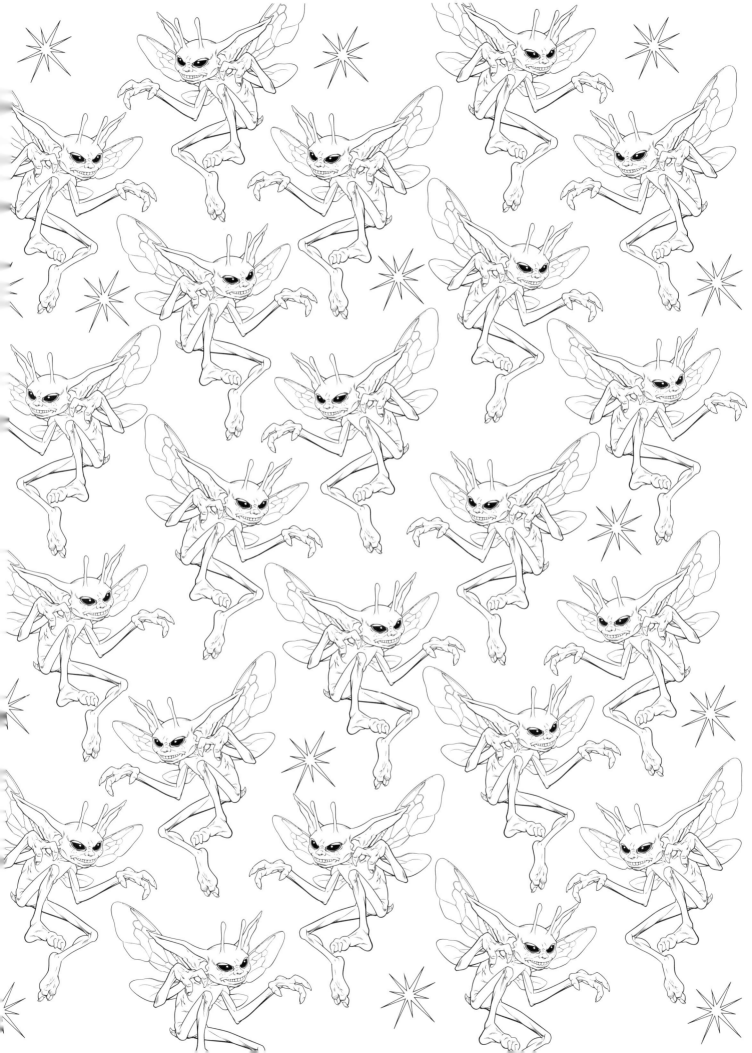

GILDEROY LOCKHART

Gadding with Ghouls
Break with a Banshee

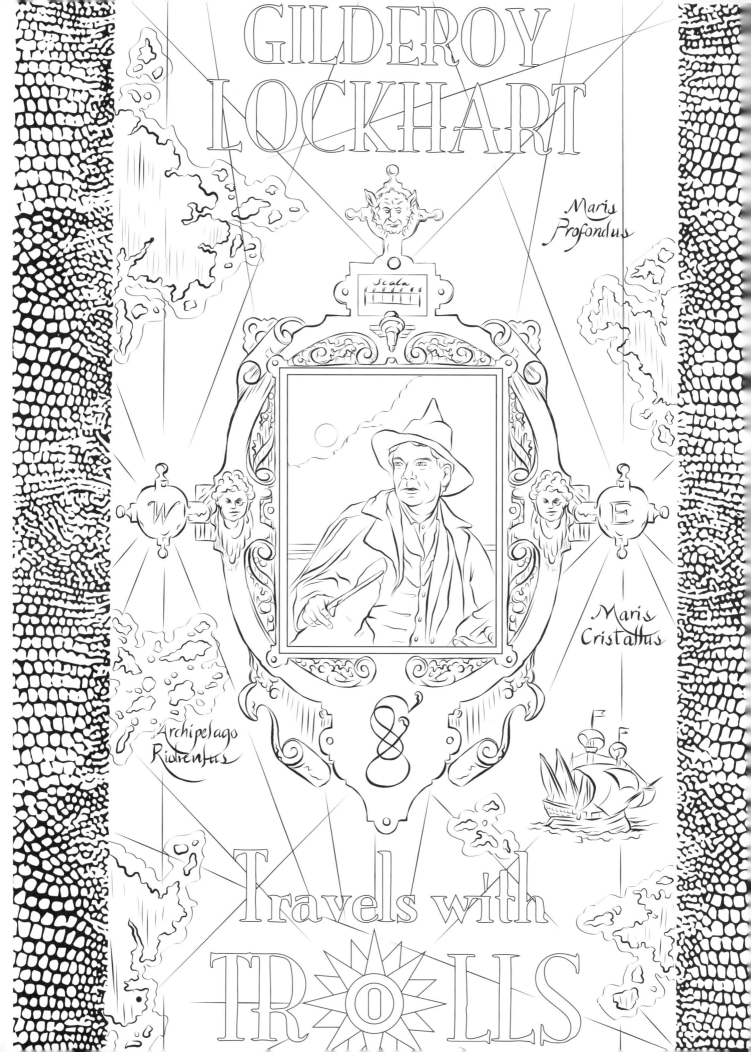

KEEP OFF THE DIRIGIBLE PLUMS

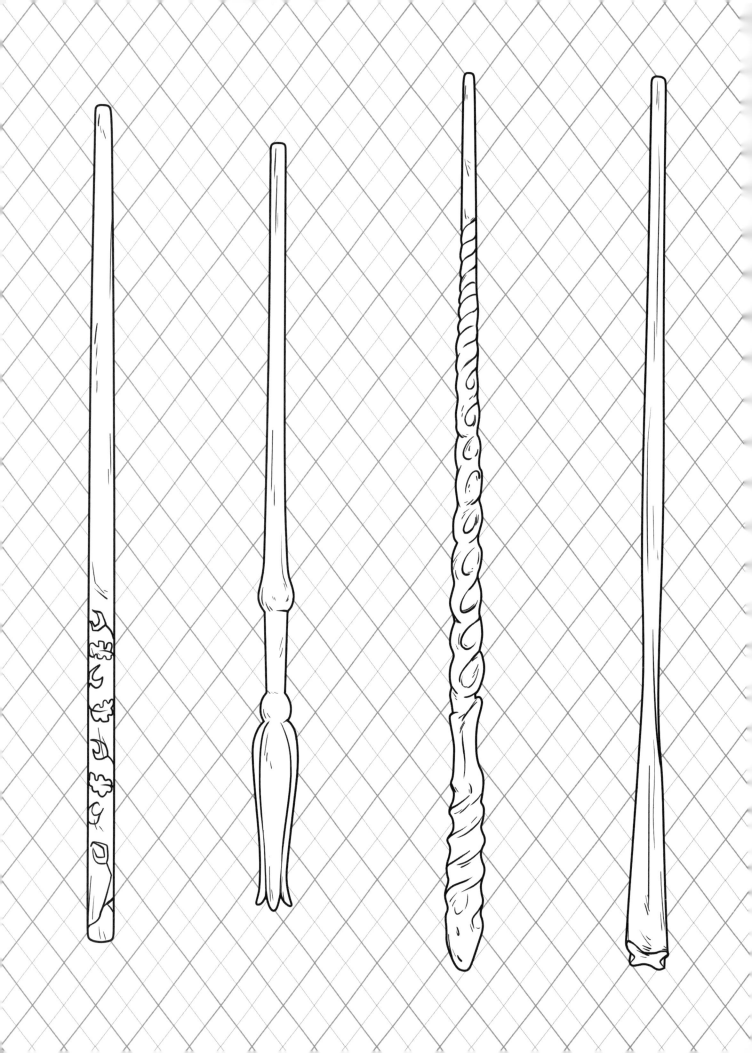

First published in the United Kingdom in 2021 by

B. T. Batsford Ltd

43 Great Ormond Street

London

WC1N 3HZ

ISBN: 9781849947473

A CIP catalogue record for this book is available from the British Library.

10 9 8 7 6 5 4 3 2 1

Publisher: Raoul Goff

VP of Licensing and Partnerships: Vanessa Lopez

VP of Creative: Chrissy Kwasnik

VP of Manufacturing: Alix Nicholaeff

Editorial Director: Vicki Jaeger

Senior Editor: Greg Solano

Design Support: Megan Sinaed-Harris and Monique Narboneta

Associate Editor: Anna Wostenberg

Senior Production Editor: Elaine Ou

Senior Production Manager: Greg Steffen

Senior Production Manager, Subsidiary Rights: Lina s Palma

Thanks to all our artists: Remie Geoffroi, Maxime LeBrun, Pablo Matamoros, Adam Raiti, Ellina Havrilov,Hend_draw from Fiverr, Tomato Farm, Conor Buckley, Paula Hanback, and Iván Fernández Silva

Insight Editions, in association with Roots of Peace, will plant two trees for each tree used in the manufacturing of this book. Roots of Peace is an internationally renowned humanitarian organization dedicated to eradicating land mines worldwide and converting war-torn lands into productive farms and wildlife habitats. Roots of Peace will plant two million fruit and nut trees in Afghanistan and provide farmers there with the skills and support necessary for sustainable land use.

Manufactured in China by Insight Editions